OPTIONS TRADING

A Comprehensive Beginner's Guide With Proven Strategies To Trade Options

Adrian McNulty

© Copyright 2018 by Adrian McNulty - All rights reserved.

It is not legal to reproduce, duplicate, or transmit any part of this document in either electronic means or in printed format. Recording of this publication is strictly prohibited.

Table Of Contents

Introduction 7

Chapter 1: Why Do You Want To Start Investing 10

Chapter 2: How To Make Sense Of The Investment World – Laying A Solid Foundation 17

Chapter 3: Steps To Investing In Stocks ....…. 31

Chapter 4: Understanding Trading Options 43

Chapter 5: Understanding The Lingo For Trading Options 49

Chapter 6: Getting Started In Trading Options 59

Chapter 7: Proven Strategies In Trading Options 71

Chapter 8: Common Trading Mistakes To Avoid 76

Conclusion 85

Introduction

Greetings readers! I would like to personally thank you for your purchase, I know there are a lot of books on the same subject and I am extremely grateful that you chose mine.

If you have the desire to become a successful options trader, you have chosen the right book. Although this is a short introduction, it will give you exactly what you need to start moving in the right direction.

The one and only reason why you are reading this book is because you want to know how to make money through trading options. Please understand that this is not a get rich quick scheme, neither is it a lottery ticket to quick success. If that is what you are looking for, you have chosen the wrong book. You are not going to make an investment today and wake up a millionaire tomorrow. First of all, you need to do a bit of work and invest some time educating yourself about it and second, you need to have some patience.

People like Warren Buffett became who they are today because of hard work. Mr Buffett is an avid reader, and states that he spends 80% of his day reading! This is the only way you are going to acquire the knowledge you need to get where you want to get in life.

People like yourself who are new to trading are afraid that the stock market will crash and that they will lose their hard earned cash. This is a healthy and rational fear; however, what people fail to understand is that whether a crash happens or not, over time you will still average approximately 10%. There is no point wasting time trying to anticipate when the next crash is going to take place. This is literally impossible, and even if there is a crash, for those who intend on trading for the long haul, it won't make much of a difference.

The main goal for the majority of people is to achieve financial independence. Today, the cost of living is so high that people barely have enough to save at the end of the month let alone achieve financial freedom. The good news is that when it comes to trading, regardless of how little you have, it is possible to make your money work for you without changing your life circumstances. Through smart trading, anyone is capable of earning a second income.

For individuals and families with a modest income becoming wealthy seems like an impossible dream. However, if you can exercise enough patience to wait for a return on your investment, investing your money can turn out to be one of the wisest decisions you will ever make.

Before we dive into the topic of trading options, let me introduce its main category: investing. Having the basics of investing will significantly help you, before you decide to take a further step into trading options.

Chapter 1: Why Do You Want To Start Investing

Most people are going to have a specific reason as to why they want to start investing, if so, you probably fall into one of the following categories:

✓ **You don't have any money but you want to make money:** The majority of people are at this position in life. Most investors don't start off rich; they start because they are fed up of being broke! You want to multiply the money that you do have but you are not sure how to go about doing so. This is possible, but it depends on whether you are able to discipline yourself enough to cut back on what you spend and start saving.

✓ **You are currently making your own investment decisions but you want to improve your skills:** You've been investing for some time and you want to increase your wealth. You have got to the point where you want to improve your skills so that you can accelerate your earning potential. The next steps that you take will depend on your goals for the next 5, 10 or 20 years.

✓ **You don't handle your own investments and you want to make more money:** You might have investment advisers or fund managers handling your investments on your behalf so that you can gain advantages on your taxes. Or you might have savings locked in with your partner in a pension fund. It may be the case that you simply don't have the time to handle your own investments. Whatever the reason, you have decided that you want to learn about the investment process for yourself so that you can either start making your own investment decisions or start to monitor what the professionals are doing with your money.

✓ **You are now in control of your pension decisions:** Unless you are a public sector employee, the chances are that you are now responsible for your pension. The funds you will have when you retire are now dependent upon what you do instead of your former employer.

How do You Handle Money?

The majority of people have got no discipline when it comes to money, by the end of the month, their bank account is empty and their credit cards are maxed out! Some people manage to save something every month, while others make wise business decisions. At this point, you need to decide whether you are a spender, a saver or an investor.

Spenders Live Lavishly

Spenders are typically people who live for the moment. Their eyes are bigger than their stomachs, and often want more than they can afford, and will borrow money to get it. Spenders don't save for the future; it isn't one of their priorities. Here are some of the main attributes of a spender; if the majority of them apply to you then you are a spender:

- ✓ The end of the month doesn't excite you.
- ✓ You are obsessed with anything new, and you will stand in a queue all night to purchase the latest Smartphone. Your friends are often left with their mouths hanging open when you tell

them how much your shoes and your handbag cost.
- ✓ You have multiple credit cards and typically use one of them to pay the bill on another credit card.
- ✓ You have an addiction for two for one offers even if you never use the spare one.
- ✓ You buy clothes you don't need.
- ✓ You always buy the first and last round of drinks without any hesitation.
- ✓ You believe in living for the moment.
- ✓ The future is a foreign concept to you.
- ✓ Sometimes you worry about money but bury your emotions by spending more.
- ✓ You buy magazines to look at the latest advertisements.

If you are a spender but you want to become an investor, you are going to have to stop spending so that you will have something to invest. However, there is hope for you yet, the fact that you are reading this book to learn about investing will provide you with an alternative on what to do with your money.

The good news is that to become a saver or an investor you don't need large sums of money. You can start saving with as little as a dollar, and you can start investing with as little as $50 per month.

Savers Always Have A Nestegg

Savers are people who want to keep their cake and eat it at a later date. A lot of savers are scared to invest; they will have thousands of dollars in the bank just for the sake of knowing that they've got thousands of dollars in the bank. Here are some attributes of a saver, if you tick most of them, you are probably a saver:

- ✓ You always have extra money at the end of the month.
- ✓ You don't do random shopping, you always have a list.
- ✓ You either don't have a credit card or you pay it off in full at the end of the month.
- ✓ You would rather wait then just buy something that you like.
- ✓ You'd rather buy something second hand then finance it and get into debt.

- ✓ Your property is more important than the contents inside it.
- ✓ You evaluate the display window at the bank.
- ✓ You keep up with interest rates.
- ✓ You don't waste anything.
- ✓ You read books on how to manage your money.

Before you become an investor, you will need to become a saver. You can become an investor and a saver, but before you invest you will need to save some money.

Investors Build Funds For The Future

Investors are builders; they want to make sure that their wealth continues to multiply. Investors want to dominate their money; they are willing to take risks as long as they know exactly what they are getting into. They want their money to work as hard for them as they worked to earn it.

You don't need an MBA in finance or a stack of money in the bank to become an investor. However, you might be able to save with your eyes closed, but this isn't the case with investing. You are going to need to know exactly what's going on with the market. You are going to need enough self discipline to be able to follow your strategy through even if you can't see anything happening. If you check the majority of the following attributes, you are an investor:

- ✓ You've got extra cash.
- ✓ You've built an emergency fund.
- ✓ You are not satisfied with what the bank is offering you.
- ✓ You strategize about how you are going to make money.
- ✓ You know enough to outsmart the charlatans.
- ✓ You are willing to trade certitude for a potentially larger reward.
- ✓ You have got enough money to be able to lock some of it away for five years.
- ✓ You know what you are doing with your money.
- ✓ You are willing to risk losing money every now and then.
- ✓ You are willing to invest your time into expanding your fortune.

Chapter 2: How To Make Sense Of The Investment World – Laying A Solid Foundation

At the most basic level, investment is exchanging something between two parties – someone who needs immediate cash so that they can invest it in something that will generate a profit in later years, and someone who has money now and doesn't need to use it until a later date. Stocks and bonds are a representation of how this type of across-time agreement is structured. Secondary markets such as the New York Stock Exchange provides investors with a platform to make cash exchanges for their investments. The intrinsic value of all investments is based on the type of income it will produce in future; this is then discounted back to the present to make up for the time value of money.

What Exactly Is An Investment

Investment is not as complicated as it has been made out to be, it is actually a very simple process. Here is a scenario to give you a better understanding.

Jack is the owner of a very successful farm; he has had many years of good farming and has enough food for his family to be able to eat for a significant amount of time. If he wanted to, he could invest some of his food for future use.

Sam has just purchased his farm and would like to spend time building the farm and a new barn so that he can develop his business and have the financial freedom that Jack has. However, he is in a bit of a bad situation because if he spends time growing the farm, he won't have time to harvest his crops for the year. This would cause Jack and his family to go hungry.

Since Sam needs to purchase extra food now so that he can produce more food later and Jack has spare food now and would like to multiply it for future use, it appears that Sam and Jack are the perfect match to make a trade. However, there are significant problems with this trade since its taking place across time. Jack wants to makes sure that his investment is not wasted and that he will get the same amount or more than what he put in. Jack is also worried that Sam will run off with his food and that he will lose out completely. At the same time he wonders if there are other farmers in the area who are in the same situation as Sam, and could give him a better deal.

Modern markets sound complicated, but they are no different than the scenario that has been presented. There are different ways that Jack and Sam can structure their arrangement, which we will look at now.

Stocks And Bonds

One of the ways that Jack and Sam can structure their arrangement is through a simple "pay you back at a later date agreement." This is the equivalent of asking someone to borrow their car, and promising to bring it back in a couple of hours. To make the deal more attractive to Jack, Sam might offer to give Jack an extra 10 pounds of wheat at the end of each year until the debt has been paid off. Going back to the car example, when you ask someone to borrow their car and offer to fill the gas tank before you bring it back, they are more likely to agree to lending it to you. So Jack would receive wheat payments each year as well as a return on his investment at the end of the loan contract.

If Sam and Jack had chosen to structure their arrangement this way, they would have created something similar to a bond. A bond is referred to as a type of debt where the debtor provides an IOU to the government or the company that they are loaning the funds from. The creditor agrees to pay interest when making payments, as well as to pay back the total amount at the end of the loan contract. Creditors make their profit from the interest paid on the original amount. In the case of Jack and Sam, if the loan term is three years and Jack loans Sam 100 pounds of wheat. Sam pays Jack back interest of 10 pounds of wheat per month over three years Jack has made a profit of three times the amount of wheat that he lent out.

Jack and Sam could have also made an arrangement where Sam borrows 100 pounds of wheat in exchange for 10% ownership in the new farm. This way, Jack would be entitled to 10% of all future profits from Sam's farm. If the farm was a success, Jack will make a positive return on his investment and make much more wheat than his original investment. If the farm doesn't succeed, he risks losing out on his investment. This type of arrangement is similar to a stock, and allows Jack and Sam to share in the risk of the project.

There are a few reasons why Jack and Sam might prefer the stock arrangement instead of the bond arrangement. For example, if the improvements that Sam wants to make on the farm are risky, he might prefer to make a stock arrangement, since the payments he would have to make to Jack would depend on the success of the business. This would eliminate any personal risk in case he was not able to make payments. Jack might prefer the stock arrangement because it gives him the chance to make more money if the farm is a success. With the bond, Jack has the security of knowing that he will get his money back as well as interest on the original loan. However, with the stock arrangement he has the potential benefit of being able to make much more wheat than his original investment.

Today, a company will issue a certificate as a stock when they do not have the funds to invest in their business, launch a new product, or build a new factory.

In exchange for providing the money they need, an investor will receive part ownership in the company. If the business is profitable in future, it will distribute its profits among investors either quarterly or annually. These payments are referred to as dividends. When an investor purchases a stock, they are given the opportunity to make a positive return on their investment over a certain period of time if the dividends received from the company are larger than the initial investment made.

Up until now, we have made the assumption that things do not change for Jack and Sam from the time they make their agreement to the time that it has been completed. Let's imagine that after Jack has given Sam the food, a swarm of wheat eating locusts attack his farm. There is now no way that Sam can make his payments, but he has the option of selling his loan to a third farmer "Daniel," who has a surplus of wheat. Daniel would give Jack his wheat back in exchange for receiving future wheat payments from Sam.

When a contract is resold in this nature, in the investment world it takes place on secondary markets such as the New York Stock Exchange. Secondary markets for financial contracts allow what was initially invested in a bond or stock to get sold to another investor. When you see prices quoted online and in newspapers for stocks and bonds, they are the recent prices that have been advertised on the secondary market.

One of the negatives associated with stocks and bonds is that most individual investors do not have the time or money to have a large portfolio. Mutual funds were born out of a solution to this problem. A mutual fund gathers money from several investors and invests their money into a larger portfolio of stocks. The portfolio is distributed between each investor; they each own a percentage and any profit made on the investment is distributed between them. A professional investor typically employed by a company such as T. Rowe Price or Fidelity will manage a mutual fund.

The Value Of An Investment
Typically, a commentator will refer to a bond as being "overvalued" or "undervalued." This description leads to the question, how is "fair value," defined? The

intrinsic value theory states that the price of an investment should not be the same value as it was to the investor who planned on holding onto it. (Although with secondary markets the majority of investors eventually sell their investments). Investors who don't plan on selling their stocks or bonds are not interested in how much the asset is worth on the secondary markets, what matters is their dividend, semi-annual or annual payments.

It seems slightly strange that a permanent dividend should have a "present value," but in terms of what is referred to as time value of money by economists, it makes perfect sense. The foundational idea is that if you receive $1 today, it will be worth more than if you received it five years from the present date. There are three different ways that you can think about this:

1. You can invest a dollar in a certificate deposit (CD) or a guaranteed bank account if you were in possession of it today.
2. The value of the dollar will go down in five years which means you will be able to do more with it today than in five years. This is due to inflation and how the cost of living rises slowly

overtime. For example, in 1970, you could buy five loafs of bread with $1, today; you wouldn't be able to buy even half a loaf of bread with $1.

3. The majority of people prefer to spend the dollar they have in their hand now as opposed to wait for five years to purchase the things they want. Most people have a preference for immediate gratification instead of delayed gratification. They would rather eat a piece of cake now instead of eating it next week.

Because future dividend payments are not worth as much as those received today, a discount rate must be applied to express their value to a rational investor.

If we are aware of the time value of money, then we can place the value of $1 today on the promise of what it will be worth five years from now. In this way, we are discounting it back to the present. If we are able to place a value on the current dollar based on the promise of $1 in the future, then it is possible to place a value on any interest or dividend payments in the future.

This is exactly what is required to value a bond, stock or any other kind of investment, estimate how much you will generate from the investment in the future, and discount it back to the present at the right time value of money.

A good way to estimate the time value for money today is to look at the interest rate on a safe investment such as a United States Treasury bond. (These are IOUs from the American government). A zero-coupon bond is a type of treasury bond, if you buy a zero-coupon bond, such as an American savings bond the amount of money you will receive at a later date is guaranteed. However, you won't get any interest payments until that time. As a result of this, a zero-coupon bond that will pay out $1 in ten years time will be a lot less than $1 today, and this is the price for the time value of money. For example, if a ten zero-coupon bond over ten years pays $50 at maturity is selling for $20 today, it then means that $50 in ten years time is the equivalent of $20 today.

Going back to the Jack and Sam example, the intrinsic value of Jacks investment is always going to be his best guess on how many pounds of wheat Sam is going to give him later on down the line. This will depend on the probability of Sam's farm being a success or not and/or how reliable he is. In the market today, intrinsic value equals the estimated future dividend or the continuous income that a company has. This is then discounted back to the present to show the time value of money and how risky the investment is likely to be.

Getting Started

What exactly does investing mean? In its simplest terms, investing means, "Putting money away to use in the future." There are thousands of investments options available to you, including bonds, stocks, exchange traded funds, mutual funds and much more. Unfortunately, for the beginner, knowing the name of an investment means nothing in comparison to the wealth of information you will need to understand to become a successful investor.

Although there are plenty of people who make a full time living out of investing, you don't have to quit your job if you don't want to. It doesn't take a lot of time to make a wise investment; if you know how to locate high quality information, and the investments that you purchase are well managed, you can leave it up to the experts. Then you can focus on what you know you are good at, make some money and have more free time to spend on what you enjoy doing the most.

One of the most important aspects of making wise investment decisions is knowing when you have enough information do get things done on your own, or when you should hire an expert. For example, it is typically more difficult to research foreign than domestic markets. Therefore, when you are making overseas investments, it's a good idea to hire someone through an exchange or mutual traded fund. This will save you a lot of time and effort.

I'm here to provide you with the information that you need to navigate your way through the complex world of investment. In the rest of this chapter, I will assist you in identifying and understanding major investments as well as their strengths and weaknesses.

The Stock Market

Stocks are shares that an investor owns in a company; they are another type of ownership investment. If you want to share in the profit and growth of a company such as McDonalds, you can. You simply purchase shares of their stock through a brokerage firm. However, even if McDonalds does make a future profit, there is no guarantee that their stocks will rise.

It's not difficult to make money on the stock market; you simply need to understand a few simple principles such as making systematic and regular investments in proven funds and companies while minimizing your investment taxes and expenses, in the long run you will make a decent return.

Trading Options

Option traders are typically independent investors, this means that they are not led by a financial advisor to handle their options trading portfolio. You take full control of the decisions and transactions that you make. If you want to become a savvy investor, options trading is the way forward. With options, making a profit is possible not matter what direction stocks are moving in. You don't need a great deal of money, and you can use options to protect gains, cut losses and control large amounts of money.

There are different types of options that are available to an investor (you will learn about them in a later chapter). As with any type of investment, you must be willing to take risks because there is no guarantee that you will make a return on your investment.

Chapter 3: Steps To Investing In Stocks

Investing in stocks is a fantastic way to build wealth. The question that every beginner wants to know is where do I start?

The short answer is that you will need to open a brokerage account; you will also need to know how much you are willing to invest as well as have a clear understanding of your financial goals. What you are not going to need is a master's degree in finance and thousands of dollars. Are you ready to go a little deeper? Here are a few steps to get you started.

What Type of Investor Are You?
Before you jump into buying stocks, it's important that you understand the different methods of approaching stock when it comes to investing. Choose the option that best reflects your current situation.

- ✓ "I'm the do it yourself type, and I'm interested in selecting stock funds and stock

for myself." Keep reading, the rest of the steps will help you. Or if you already understand how stock buying works, all you need is to find yourself a good brokerage.

✓ **I believe that stocks are a good investment, but I'd rather someone else manage the process for me."** Robo-advisors provide low cost investment management. They will ask you some questions, all you have to do is answer them and they will handle the rest of the process.

Choose Between Stock Mutual Funds And Stocks

For the majority of people, investing in stocks means making a choice between these two investment types.

- **Individual Stocks:** If you want to invest in a specific company you can purchase a few shares to test the waters. It is possible to build a diversified portfolio out of several individual stocks, but it takes a significant investment.
- **Stock, exchange traded funds or mutual funds:** Mutual funds allow you to purchase small pieces of several different stocks in one transaction. ETFs and index funds track an

index; an example of this is a Standard and Poor 500 fund. It mimics that index by purchasing the stock of the companies in it. Your investment into the fund means that you own a small portion of those companies. You can build a diversified portfolio by putting several funds together.

The benefit of stock mutual funds is that they are known for being diversified and so this reduces your risk. However, they are unlikely to rise at an extensive rate the way some individual stocks do. The benefit of individual stocks is that if you are wise in your choice, you can make a lot of money. There is a very slim chance of becoming rich from one individual stock. For the majority of investors, especially those who are investing for retirement, developing a portfolio made up of mainly mutual funds is the better choice.

What Is Your Budget?

This question is often asked in two parts by new investors:

1. **Is there a certain amount that I need to get the ball rolling?** The amount of money required to invest in stocks individually will depend on how expensive the shares are. If you have expensive tastes, but don't have much money to invest, a broker that provides fractional shares (pieces of stocks) may be best for you. If you are interested in mutual funds but you don't have a large budget, your best bet might be an ETF. All mutual funds, even index funds have a minimum of $1000 or more, but ETFs are similar to stocks and they trade the same. This means that instead of a fund minimum, you purchase them for a share price.

2. **Is there are certain amount that I should invest?** If your investments are through funds, you can allocate quite a substantial portion of your portfolio towards stock funds, particularly if you intend on investing for the long term. A 25 year old investing for retirement may have 70% of their portfolio in stock funds and the remainder in bond funds. Individual stocks are another issue; I recommend that you keep them to 10% or less of your investment portfolio.

This is because there is more risk associated with individual stock trading. The fund diversification isn't built in to the individual stock; you have to put more effort into it.

Open an Account

If you are funding a retirement plan such as a 401(k) through your workplace, there is a possibility that you already have a mutual fund investment. If you are not investing into a 401(k), or you find that you don't have very many investment choices, you can purchase stocks through an online broker. You can open an individual retirement account, also known as an IRA account. If you have already reached your retirement goals you can open a taxable brokerage account.

If you are planning on opening a new account, find a broker that has low account minimums as well as low fees. The majority of brokers provide a list of no transaction fee mutual funds or commission free ETFs. This will protect you against charges every time you buy or sell. When dealing with individual stocks, you should expect to pay $5 to $10 per trade; however, this depends on the broker. There are a few free services such as the Robinhood app.

You will need to consider the following when comparing brokers:

- **Research resources:** Accurate information on leading companies can put your stock buying into alignment. A lot of the top brokers offer this service.
- **Educational resources:** As a beginner, tutorials and guides produced by the broker can be of great help. They can help you to get a better understanding of the buying process.
- **Customer support:** A good broker provides customer support through several different channels including online chat, email and phone.
- **Trading platform:** All broker websites allow you to buy stock; however, if you plan on doing this on a regular basis, you might want to upgrade to a more user friendly system.

Do Your Research

It's never a good idea to go into anything with your eyes closed, especially when it comes to partying with your hard earned cash. Regardless of whether or not you will be using a broker, it is advised that you are familiar with the investment process so that you don't get ripped off. Please bear in mind that it is impossible to predict what the market is going to do, but you can do as much research as possible to ensure that you are making an informed decision. This means that you will need to research things such as annual company reports, recent news about a company, analyst ratings, and past performance. Your broker's website should be able to provide you with this type of information.

With index mutual funds or ETFs, it is not as important to research how an individual fund is performing. What you will need to understand are the fees and whether your investment goals can be met by the fund. Since these funds are a replica of the stock index, their performance will be closely aligned with that benchmark, and funds that track the same benchmark should mirror each other.

It is your responsibility to work out the type of funds and the stocks that lie behind those funds so that you can decide whether or not you want to include them in your portfolio. If you are interested in small companies, you may want to do some research on Russell 2000 funds, if you are interested in large American companies you might want to research S&P 500 index funds.

You will then need to make a comparison between funds that track similar benchmarks by their fees. Each fund will list its expense ratio clearly, the amount of your investment that goes towards the funds yearly operating costs. This number should be under 0.25%, although it might be higher for niche funds.

Stay In Control Of Your Emotions

This is probably the most difficult thing about investing. Prepare yourself to see large swings in share prices attached to general market turmoil, company news and a host of other issues. There is a lot of emotion involved in investing and people can easily get carried away. It's easy to get scared and abandon the investment at the wrong time, or get too excited when things are going well and invest more than you had budgeted for. No matter how emotional you get, it's important to remain focused and stick to the long term plan that you have.

You will need to know the price you will want to invest at and how far you are willing to allow stock to lose their value before you sell. Setting rules as well as selecting the right type of order when you place a trade will minimize your risk and help you to combat your emotional responses.

Tips For Investing In Stocks
- **Make a plan:** If you don't know where you are going, getting there is going to be difficult. What are your reasons for investing and when do you expect to see a return on your investment? How much can you afford to spare? These are the questions you should be asking yourself when you are making a plan.
- **Diversify Your Investments:** Purchase stocks in different companies so that you are not

dependant on one for a return on your investment.

- **Avoid Leverage:** Leverage means that you use borrowed money to make your investments. The bottom line is if you can't afford to invest then don't. If the market doesn't work in your favour, you will end up in even more debt than you started out with.
- **Educate Yourself:** This might sound like common sense, but you will be surprised at the amount of people who just jump into investing head first without fully understanding it. You will save yourself a lot of time and money if you take some time out to educate yourself about investing.

Understanding The Lingo Of The Stock Market

The investment process is hard enough, but if you are unable to understand the language used on the stock market, it can make it almost impossible to get your foot in the door. There are a lot of technical terms you will need to understand, here are the most common:

Averaging Down: When an investor purchases more of a stock as the price decreases it is referred to as averaging down. This process causes the average purchase price to decrease.

Bear Market: When the stock market is in a down trend, it is referred to as a bear market.

Blue Chip Stocks: These are the most successful companies in an industry. They provide a stable record of consistent dividend payments and have a reputation for good fiscal management.

Bull Market: When the entire stock market is in an extended period of increasing stock prices. It is opposite to the bear market.

Exchange: This is the location where investments are traded. The most well known in America is the New York Stock Exchange.

Initial Public Offering (IPO) The first offering or sale of a stock by a company to the public. The stock is not owned by an inside or private investor.

Order: When an investor places their bid to buy or sell a certain number of stocks. To buy or sell 100 shares of stock, you are required to put in an order.

Quote: The latest information on a stocks trading price. There is sometimes a 20 minute delay unless you are trading from a brokers trading platform.

Rally: A speedy increase in the price of a stock or the overall price level of the market.

Sector: When a group of stocks are a part of the same industry. For example, Nike and Adidas are a part of the retail industry.

Spread: This is the difference between the ask price and the bid is referred to as the spread.

Volume: The amount of shares of stock prices traded during a certain time period. This is typically measured in average daily trading volumes.

Yield: The yield typically refers to how much profit was made from an investment. This is worked out by dividing the yearly dividend amount by the price that the stock was purchased for.

Chapter 4: Understanding Trading Options

Options are viewed as a derivative form of security because its price is based on the price of another asset. An option is a contract giving traders the right to purchase or sell an underlying asset at a fixed price before or on a particular date. A call option gives the individual the right to buy and a put option enables the individual to sell. There is a slight difference between forwards or futures, and that is that they give you the obligation and the right to both buy and sell options.

Put And Call Options

A call option can be seen as a deposit that can be used at a later date. For example, if a land developer has seen a piece of land, he might not want to purchase it now but later on in the future. However, he will only want to use that right if the right zoning laws have been implemented. The developer can purchase the call option through the owner of the land from a set price at any time within a 3 year time frame. To secure this; the developer will have to pay a deposit so that the landowner knows that he is serious. This is referred to as a premium and it is how much the options contract will cost. Within two years, the zoning laws have been put in place, the developer chooses to purchase the land for the agreed price even though the there has been an increase in the market value of the land. Alternatively, if approval for zoning isn't granted in the specified time period the developer will have to pay the market price. Even if he is unable to pay it, the landowner is entitled to keep the deposit.

Alternatively, a put option is similar to an insurance policy. The land developer has several pieces of expensive land and is concerned that the economy isn't doing so well. He wants to lock his portfolio in so that if there is a bear market his loses won't exceed more than 10% of its value. To do this he can buy a put option that allows him to put the index back on the market at any time during the two year period. If there is a market crash of 20% within the next six months his maximum loss will be 10% because of his put option. It is important to mention that if there is no drop in the market over the two year period, the land developer will lose his premium.

There are some important points to take from these examples. When you purchase an option, you are not obligated to, but you have the right to do what you want to do with it. You can choose to allow the expiration date to pass, which will mean that the option no longer has any value. At this point, you won't earn anything from your investment but will lose what you put in. It is also important to mention that an option is nothing but a contract that handles an underlying asset. This puts an option in the class of a derivative. Options are typically traded on a range of financial securities such as commodities, foreign currencies and bonds.

Calls And Puts: Understanding Cardinal Coordinates

You are given a long position in the market when you own a call option. When you own a put option, you are given a short position in the market. When you sell a put, you are given a long position. It is essential that these four things are kept straight as they have an effect on the four things you can do with an option. Buy puts, sell puts, buy calls and sell calls.

Those who buy options are referred to as holders, and those who sell options are referred to as writers of options. There is an important difference between the buyer and seller:

- There is no obligation for a put holder to do anything with their options. They don't have to buy or sell. This puts a limitation on the risks of buyer options so that their maximum loss is their options premiums.
- Put and call writers are obligated to take action with their stocks, they are required to either buy or sell. This means that there is a possibility that a buyer or a seller is obligated to buy or sell. There is also an implication that there is an unlimited risk associated with option sellers. This means that there is a chance that they can lose a lot more than the actual price of the options premium.

If the share price is higher than the strike price, the option is referred to as "In the money." When the share price is less than the strike price, a put option is considered in the money. The intrinsic value is how much the share price is in the money. If the underlying price remains less than the strike price for a call, or more than the strike price for a put, the option is said to be "Out of the money." An option is referred to as "At the money," when the underlying price is close to or near the strike price.

As previously mentioned, the price of an option is referred to as a premium. There are several factors that determine this price such as volatility, time value, strike price and stock price. As a result of these factors, it is difficult to determine the premium of an option.

Despite the fact that employee options are only available to employees, they can be viewed as a type of call option. A lot of companies use stock options in an attempt to attract and keep the employees with the most potential, this is especially true when it comes to management. They have some similarities to regular stock options in that an employee is not obligated to purchase company stock; however, they do have a right to. The contract only exists between the company and the employee which means that it can't be exchanged with anyone else. A regular option is not tied to a company and can be traded between anyone.

Chapter 5: Understanding The Lingo For Trading Options

Before you can successfully trade options, you will need to understand the terminology that is associated with it. Here is a list of some of the most common terms used in options trading:

Accumulation: When stocks begin moving in a sideways direction after there has been a large drop once investors start to accumulate.

Adjusted Options: Stock options that have been non-standardized with customized terms. The aim of this process is to factor in the major changes to the underlying stock capital into the price.

All or None Order (AON): This is an order that must be filled completely before it can be executed. This order is helpful to traders wishing to execute an option strategy that is complex but needs to be filled precisely.

American Style Option: This type of option contract can be actioned at any time between the purchase and the expiration date. American style is used for the majority of exchange trade options.

Ask Price: This is the price that the person selling is willing to sell for. Stocks and option contracts are purchased on their ask price.

Back Month: An option spread that has got two expiration months. If the months are September and December, the back month will be December because it is the month that is farthest away.

Beta: A number that indicates how a stock price typically moves within the stock market.

Bid Price: A trader sells at the bid price when a potential buyer wants to buy from you.

Binary Options: These options either provide you with a fixed term payment or they don't pay anything at all.

Breakout: This process takes place when a stock price or average travels above a prior high resistance or prior low support level. The trend tends to continue in this direction.

Call Ratio Spread: A trading strategy that involves credit options. It enables traders to make a profit when the stock increases, decreases or goes sideways through additional shorting of the money calls as opposed to the money calls that have been bought.

Called Away: This process is when the call option writer has an obligation to give up the underlying stock option to the buyer at the same price as the strike price of the call option.

Call Options: These options provide the holder with the right to purchase the underlying security at an agreed price for a certain period of time that has been fixed.

Capitalization: The total number of securities that have been provided by a corporation. This might include surplus, common stock, preferred stock, debentures and bonds.

Commission: The fee that the brokerage firm will charge a trader to use its services.

Day Order: If an order is not executed, it will expire at the end of the day.

Day Trader: Traders who spend the day opening and closing option or multiple option positions.

Debit: Money or expenses that have been paid out from an account. When the net cost is more than the proceeds of the net sale it is referred to as a debit transaction.

Deliverables: When the options are exercised, financial assets are given to the option holders.

Discount: If an option is trading for a lower price than its intrinsic value, it is referred to as a discount.

Dividend: When shareholders are paid a share of a company's profits.

Equity Option: When the underlying security of an option is common stock.

Expiration Date: The day that an option contract is no longer valid.

Expiration Time: The expiration date has an expiration time; the exercise notice must be submitted by that time.

Extrinsic Value: This is also referred to as "Time Value" or "Premium Value." It is the difference between the price of an option and its intrinsic value.

Financial Instrument: An electronic or physical document that either transfers value or has intrinsic monetary value. For example, precious metals, options, futures, shares and cash are all financial instruments.

Front Month: An option spread that has two expiration months. If the months are June and October, the front month will be June.

Front Spreads: Options strategies that have been designed so that they profit from the neutral market conditions where prices don't change often.

Fundamental Analysis: A method used to analyze the prospects of a security by evaluating the accepted measures of accounting through measures such as assets, sales and earnings.

Goldilock Economy: When an economy has moderate inflation and steady growth which is neither too hot nor too cold.

Going Forward: Analysts use this term, it means "In the future."

Greeks: A mathematical strategy that is used to calculate stock and option prices.

Grocession: An extended period of growth of approximately 0 to 2% in GDP that will appear like a recession.

Hedge: A compensatory price movement that protects transactions against loss.

Horizontal Spread: An option strategy where the options have the same strike price with a different expiration date.

Index: A group of prices that have several common entities that have been generated into one number.

Index Option: When the underlying asset of an option is an index as opposed to a hard asset. The majority of index options are cash based.

Limit Order: An order to purchase or sell securities at an agreed price.

Liquidity: How easily a sale or purchase can be made without having an effect on the existing market price.

Long: When something is owned.

Margin: To purchase security through a loan from a brokerage house. The margin requirement is set by the Federal Reserve board and it is the investments maximum percentage that the brokerage firm can loan out.

Market Order: An order to purchase or sell securities at the present market place. As long as there is a market for the security the order will be filled.

Mini Options: Stock options that are only covered by 10 shares as opposed to 1000.

NASFAQ: This is the acronym for National Association of Securities Dealers Automatic Quotation System. Securities are listed in the United States through an electronic market place and it is here that they are electronically traded.

Narrow Based: This typically refers to an index, it is an indication that the index is made up of a limited number of stocks.

Neutral: This describes an option that is neither bullish nor bearish. Neutral option strategies are typically designed to perform at their best when there is a minimal or no net change in the underlying stock price.

Non-Equity Option: When the underlying entity of an option is not common stock. This generally refers to physical commodity options. It can also be extended to include index options.

One Sided Market: When there are either more sellers than buyers on a market or more buyers than sellers.

Option: The right to buy or sell certain securities at a certain price during a certain time. A put enables the holder to sell the stock. A call enables a person to buy the stock.

Physical Option: When the underlying security of an option is not futures or stock but a physical commodity. The physical commodity is generally a treasury debt issue or a currency.

Profit Table: A certain strategy that has been arranged in a table of results. This is typically drawn on a profit graph in a tabular compilation.

Quarterlies: Options that have an expiration cycle every quarter.

Resistance: A technical analysis term that indicates a price area that is higher than the price of the current stock where there is excess supply for the stock. This can lead to the stock finding it difficult to rise through the price.

Reverse Hedge: This is also referred to as a synthetic straddle, it is a strategy where the underlying stock is sold short and then calls are purchased on more shares than he has sold short.

Selling Climax: An extremely heavy volume that is created when investors panic and dump their stock. This is a good time to buy because it generally marks the end of a bear market.

Short Option: A position that results from making an opening sale or writing of a put contract or a call, which is then taken care of in a brokerage account.

Swing Trading: A form of trading where short term price swings are traded for short term profits.

Technical Analysis: The method that is used to predict the price of future stock movements based on the how stock price movements have operated previously.

Trend: The direction that a price movement takes. Until there is a clear change, it is assumed that a trend in motion remains intact.

Uncovering Option: When an investor doesn't have a position that corresponds with the underlying security a written option is considered uncovered.

Volatile: A market or stock that moves up or down drastically or unexpectedly.

Write: When an option is shorted. This is the process of creating a new contract for an option and selling it through the sell to open order.

Chapter 6: Getting Started In Trading Options

Open A Brokerage Account

The first thing you will need to do if you want to start trading options is to open a brokerage account. You can either open an account online or use a traditional account with a broker. Here is some advice to follow before opening a brokerage account:

- Commissions will vary between brokerage accounts; therefore, make sure that you compare prices before making a commitment. There are some firms where no commission is required, but that might mean that you have to make up the price elsewhere so make sure you do your research properly.
- Once you have made a short list of the brokerage companies that you are interested in, do some research through online reviews and forums where you can speak to other traders

who have used the brokerages you are interested in. Conducting effective research is an easy way to avoid some of the pitfalls that others have fallen into.
- Unfortunately, there are many unscrupulous people who have set up scam sites. This is why it's important to do your research before making a financial commitment.
- You will need to open a margin account if you want to sell options. A cash account will only allow you to buy options.
- Visit the website of the broker you are considering and look for a guided tour of its tools and platform. Video tutorials and screenshots are great, but you can get a better idea of the broker through a simulated trading platform. When looking at a website you will need to decide whether it is user friendly, if not you might want to look for another broker. If a website is difficult to use, it's an indication of the service you are likely to get from the broker. How easy is it to place a trade? Does the platform provide everything you need to be a successful trader? Is the website reliable? How

long does it take to load up? What type of platform fee does the broker charge? Is it monthly or annual?

- Online trading can leave you vulnerable to cyber criminals wanting to steal your details. Make sure that the brokerage you choose has a secure payment gateway, or that they use a third party payment system such as PayPal or Payoneer.

Getting Approval

Before you can start buying or selling options, you will need approval from your brokerage house. The brokerage firm that handles your account will set a limit based upon the amount of funds available and your experience. The requirements for each firm are different, but their main aims are to make sure that their customers know what they are doing and that they understand the risks associated with trading. If you don't have an options account, you won't be able to write covered calls.

- Covered call writing involves selling the right to purchase your stock during the option term at a strike price. The buyer and not the seller has the right, the stock must remain in the brokerage account and it can't be transferred or sold while the call is outstanding.
- Options are basically short term investments. If you want to earn a decent return, you will need to pay attention to price movements of the optioned security. In order to accurately predict the price movements you will need to have an understanding of the basics of technical analysis.
- Support and resistance levels are points at which the stock don't drop below (support) or rise above (resistance). Support is when there are high purchase levels at a certain point. Resistance is where there are consistently high purchase levels at a certain price.
- When a stock is moving in a certain direction and it is being pushed by a lot of volume, this is generally a signal that there is a strong trend and there may be a chance of making a lot of money.

- History will often repeat itself; this is also true of stock prices. You will need to pay attention to specific patterns when it comes to stock price movement. This will give you an indication of the direction that the stock price is headed.

The Core Elements Of Options Trading

An option is basically a contract enabling you to buy or sell a stock at a negotiated price by a certain date. Before you place the trade, there are three choices you will need to make:

1. Make a decision about the direction that you think the stock will move in.
2. Make a prediction about how low or high the stock will move from the price that it's at now.
3. Work out when you think the stock is likely to move.

If you think the price of a stock is going to go up, purchase a call option. If you think the price of a stock is going to go down, purchase a put option.

An option is only valuable if the price of the stock closes the expiration period of the option. It should either be higher or lower than the strike price. It is advised that you purchase your option at a strike price that mirrors where you anticipate the stock will be during the lifetime of the option.

There is an expiration date on every option; however, you can't just decide on a random date. The option chain will give you a choice of what's available. The riskiest options are the daily and weekly options and should be left to the options traders with more experience. If you are planning on investing for the long term, a monthly or yearly expiration date is advised. The longer your expiration date, the more time your stock has to move so that you see a return on your investment.

Another advantage of having a longer expiration date is that the option is able to retain time value, regardless of whether the stock price trades for less than the strike price. As the expiration date approaches, the value of an option starts to decrease. No investor wants to watch their stocks decline before their eyes! If a trade doesn't work in the best interest of an investor, they can still make a profit according to the time value that is left on the option. If the option contract is longer, this is more likely.

Assess The Depth, Breath And Cost Of Tools And Data

Research and data are an options trader's lifeblood. Here are some of the things you should look out for:

- Quote feeds that are frequently updated.
- Basic charting to help you chose your entry and exit points.
- The ability to evaluate the potential risks and rewards of a trade.
- Screening tools.

If you are looking to advance into the more expert trading strategies, you will need trade with analytical modeling tools that are a bit deeper. These include, the ability to track, test and build trading strategies. You will want to check whether any of the extra features cost more. There might be some professional level tools available to customers who meet certain account balance minimums.

Paper Trading

It's easy to get excited about trading; however, it is essential that you are fully acquainted with the process before you jump in head first. Before you start risking your hard earned money, you can start with paper trading. This is basically pretend trading, you can either use practice trading software or enter pretend trades into a spreadsheet. Spend a few months evaluating your returns, if you find that you are making decent returns, start working your way into real trading, but do so slowly.

Paper trading is significantly different to real trading because there are no commissions involved, and neither is there any psychological pressure. Even though there is no way of predicting real results, paper trading is a good way to learn the mechanics of trading.

Limit Orders

You don't want to waste money paying market prices for options because the price of execution might be higher than expected. You can avoid this by using limit orders to name your price; this will ensure that your return is maximized.

Periodically Reevaluate Your Strategy

The market is constantly changing, nothing ever stays the same. Therefore, if you want to keep up you are going to have to reevaluate your strategy every so often. If certain strategies didn't work out for you, try something else, but you should also make sure that you repeat the strategies that were of most benefit to you. Instead of diversifying, it is advised that you focus on a few positions. If you are going to include options in your investment portfolio it shouldn't make up more than 10 percent of it.

Advanced Trading Options

If you want to improve your skills as a trader, join an online forum and learn from some of the experts who have been successfully trading for years. You should also bear in mind that behind every success story there is failure. Becoming a successful trader is not easy; you are going to have to learn some painful lessons before you succeed. However, you can avoid a hard fall by learning from the mistakes of other traders.

Think About Other Strategies

Once you have had a certain level of success, you are eligible to take on some more complex strategies for trading options. You can get some practice through paper trading so that you will find it easier when you start trading in real time. Here are some strategies that you might want to consider:

- **The Straddle:** This strategy involves purchasing a call and put option at the same maturity date and strike price so that your exposure is limited. This strategy works best when the market isn't moving in a single

direction but up and down. There is also the risk that only one side of the market will provide the highest returns.
- **The Strip:** This strategy is similar to the straddle; however, when you are on a downward price movement there is a high chance of making double the money.

Study The Greeks

Once you have learned the ins and outs of simple options trading and you have decided to take bigger risks, you can learn about the Greeks. Traders use these metrics to maximize their returns:

- **Delta:** How much an option price moves in relation to how much the price of the underlying asset moves.
- **Gamma:** The rate that delta changes based on the stock price changing by a $1.
- **Theta:** This is referred to as the option prices "time decay." It measures how much the prices go down the closer it gets to the expiration of the option.

- **Vega:** How much the option price changes based on how volatile the underlying asset is.

Some Helpful Tips To Keep In Mind

- Before you make a financial investment, practice paper trading.
- Make sure you are prepared for a margin call if you trade margins.
- If you can't afford to lose your money, don't trade.
- Never spend more than 10% of your savings on trading options.

Chapter 7: Proven Strategies In Trading Options

The majority of investors in search of effective strategies for trading options have got the wrong idea. They look for tricks, and gimmicks that they hope will definitely work for them. The word "definitely," in options trading or in any kind of investment for that matter doesn't exist.

The best investment vehicle around are options. They give investors the opportunity to take a long, short or a neutral position. They give you the ability to effectively manage risk more so than any other method of investment. If you use them wisely, they will be good to you. Here are some tips to help you succeed as an options trader.

Covered Call

Outside of buying a naked call option, you can also take part in a buy-write or a covered call strategy. With this strategy you would make an outright purchase of the assets at the same time as writing a call option on the purchased assets. The amount of assets you own should be the same as the amount of assets underlying the call option. When investors hold a neutral opinion of the asset and a short term position and they are looking to increase their profit margins, they will use a covered call.

Married Put

An investor who buys or owns a certain asset (such as shares) will buy a put option for the same number of shares. This strategy is used by investors when the asset price is bullish, and they want to protect themselves against short-term potential losses. This strategy works in the same way as an insurance policy. It will establish a floor if the asset price makes a significant drop which means that you will only lose a certain amount of money.

Bull Call Spread

An investor will buy an option at a certain strike price, and sell the same amount of calls at a strike price of a higher value. The expiration month and underlying asset for both call options will be the same. An investor will use this type of strategy with a bullish asset and he expects the price of the underlying asset to rise moderately.

Bear Put Spread

This is another type of vertical spread that is similar to the bull call spread. The investor will buy options at a certain strike price and sell the same amount of puts at a reduced strike price. Both options would have the same expiration date and the same underlying asset. This is a strategy that is used when the trader is bearish and expects a price decline in the underlying asset. It offers both a limited amount of losses and gains.

Protective Collar

Writing an out of the money call option and purchasing an out of the money put option for the same underlying share at the same time is referred to as a protective collar. Investors often use this strategy after there have been substantial gains after a long position on a stock. This enables investors to lock in profits without having to sell their shares.

Long Straddle

When an investor buys a put option and a call option at the same strike price, expiration date and underlying asset, it is referred to as a long straddle. This strategy is often used when an investor feels that there is going to be a significant price move of the underlying asset but is uncertain as to which direction the move will take. This strategy enables investors to maintain unlimited gains at the same time as limiting the loss on the cost of both option contracts.

Butterfly Spread

When an investor combines both bear and bull spread strategies and three different strike prices are used it is known as a butterfly spread.

Iron Condor

The iron condor is when the investor holds a short and long position in two different strangle strategies. It is not the easiest strategy to learn and you will need to spend some time practicing to get the full understanding of it.

Iron Butterfly

The investor either combines a short or a long straddle with the simultaneous sale or purchase of a strangle. Although there are similarities to the butterfly spread strategy, it is different because it uses both puts and calls as opposed to using either one of them. There is a specific range that profit and loss are both limited to, but this will depend on the strike prices of the options. Investors cut costs and limit risks by using out of the money options.

Chapter 8: Common Trading Mistakes To Avoid

If you don't make mistakes in life you will never learn. However, there is such thing as common sense, and there are certain mistakes that you can definitely afford to avoid. It's impossible to be a flawless investor; however, understanding some of the common investment errors will save you a lot of time and money.

Using Too Much Margin

When an investor borrows money to purchase securities it is referred to as margin. It can assist you in making more money, but one of the major downsides is that it can cause you to lose a great deal of money.

As a new investor, the worst thing you can do is get too enthusiastic about what appears to look like free money. If you use margin and your investment is unsuccessful, you will end up in debt with nothing to show for it. The question is, would you purchase stocks on your credit card? I am hoping that everyone reading this answered no. When you overuse margin, you are essentially doing the same as buying stocks on your credit card, despite the fact that the interest rate is not as high.

Using margin also requires you to closely monitor your positions because of the high losses and gains associated with small price movements. If you are unable to keep a close watch on your positions, and make decisions about your positions and there is a drop, your brokerage firm will recover any losses you have accrued by selling your stock. This is something that you definitely want to avoid.

It is wise that you use margin as little as possible as a new investor. Only use it if you are completely knowledgeable of the risk involved. Using margins can force you into selling your positions at the bottom; this is where you should be in the market waiting for things to turn around in your favor.

Listening To The Wrong People

The majority of investors make this mistake at some point in their career. You might hear friends or relatives talking about stocks that they have heard are about to start earning a lot, or the stock is about to get bought out, or that a ground breaking new product is about to be released. Even if the information they have provided is true, it does not necessarily mean that you should jump on the bandwagon and call your broker to trade for you.

You will also hear these tips from investment professionals either online or on TV. They will talk about the stock as if it's the next big buy, when really it was just the flavor of that day. The majority of these stock tips are not accurate and will often collapse as soon as you have bought them. Buying stocks that you hear about in the media is often no more than a speculative gamble.

This doesn't mean that you should shy away from every stock tip; however, if something really catches your attention, evaluate the source that the information is coming from. You will then need to do your homework, do your research and find out what you are buying and why.

Day Trading

Day trading is not the best option if you are thinking about becoming an active trader. Unless you are a seasoned investor, stay away from it because it is a dangerous game. As well as being investment savvy, there is special equipment that a successful day trader requires that is generally not available to the average trader. Did you know that a day trading workstation can cost an estimated $50,000? You will also need the same amount of money to trade and maintain an efficient strategy.

It is impossible to start day trading with the extra $5,000 that you have in the bank. One of the main reasons for this is the need for speed. The systems that online brokers use are not fast enough to provide a true day trader with the service that he requires. In fact, day trading is considered to be such a difficult practice that the majority of brokerages that provide day trading accounts expect investors to get a formal trading qualification.

Common Option Trading Mistakes To Avoid

As a new trader, there are times when you are going to feel overwhelmed. One of the many advantages of trading options is that it provides you with several different ways that you can take advantage of how you think the direction of the underlying security will move in. If you are going to make better option trading decisions, it is important that you avoid certain mistakes, here are some of them.

Your Outlook And Strategy Don't Match

When you start trading options, it's important that you are able to develop an outlook for what you anticipate will happen. To begin with you can use either fundamental analysis, or technical analysis or a combination of both to develop an outlook.

Fundamental analysis is when a company is evaluated on the following factors:

- Current business trends
- Performance data
- Financial statements

An outlook is made up of how long you think it will take before your idea is a success and directional bias.

Technical analysis is when market action is interpreted in terms of price and volume. This information is recorded on a chart and the following areas are evaluated:

- Resistance
- Areas of support
- Potential buy/sell opportunities

As you evaluate the various options strategies that are available, it is important that the strategy you choose lines up with the outlook you are expecting.

Choosing The Wrong Expiration
When it comes to deciding on an expiration date there are several that you can choose from. The good news is that if you are capable of developing an outlook, then it won't be as difficult to choose the best expiration date.

A simple checklist can help when it comes to choosing an expiration date. Here are some of the things that you will need to pay attention to:

- The length of time it will take before the trade plays out.
- Do you want to keep hold of the trade through a stock split, an earnings announcement or other events?
- Do you have enough liquidity to support your trade?

Not Choosing The Right Position Size

Fear and greed are the two emotions that lead to choosing the wrong position size. If you make decisions out of greed, you run the risk of trading a position size that is too big for your account size. This might happen when a trade goes against the outlook and then you have to suffer the consequences of a loss. On the other hand, fear can cause you not to invest enough which means that you miss out on a decent return on your investment.

When you decide on the trade size, it is important that you are comfortable with how much you stand to lose if the trade is unsuccessful. The ideal trade size is big enough to benefit the account, but small enough that you are not worried about a loss.

Ignoring Probability

When you are deciding to place a trade, it is important that you take into account the probabilities of your strategy. Not only does it give you an idea of what is likely to happen statistically, but it is also essential to helping you understand if it makes sense to take the risk.

Failure to Plan

A good trading plan will help you to avoid many of the common mistakes made by traders. These are the things you should consider when making a trading plan:

- What financial risk are you willing to take for each trade?

- How do you intend on searching for opportunities in the market place?
- When do you plan on entering the trade?
- What type of exit strategy do you have?

As previously mentioned, greed and fear can cause you to make irrational decisions that you wouldn't make under normal circumstances. The main advantage of having a trading plan is that it helps to separate your emotions from your trading. It also gives you a process that you can replicate in future. Without a plan it can become difficult to improve your skills as a trader.

Conclusion

Thank you once again for choosing to buy my book and thank you even more for reading it all the way through. My hope is that you are now confident enough to start trading and that you reach your financial goals. I just want you to remember that this isn't a get rich quick scheme. Unless you are one of the lucky ones, don't expect to become an overnight millionaire. It is going to take hard work and persistence. The market is always changing; a good strategy doesn't stay the same forever. Just because it worked for you today, doesn't mean it's going to work for you tomorrow. Therefore, you are going to have to keep up to date with the latest trends and keep an eye on the market.

I wish you every success in your investing endeavours!

www.ingramcontent.com/pod-product-compliance
Lightning Source LLC
Chambersburg PA
CBHW070347230526
45471CB00006B/2458